If You Lived During the American Revolution

Library of Congress Cataloging-in-Publication Data Available
ISBN 978-1-338-84565-5 (paperback) / 978-1-338-84566-2 (hardcover)

10 9 8 7 6 5 4 3 2 1 26 27 28 29 30
Printed in China 38
First edition, February 2026
Book design by Jaime Lucero and Brian LaRossa

If You Lived During the American Revolution

Written By
Chris Newell

Illustrated By
Steffi Walthall

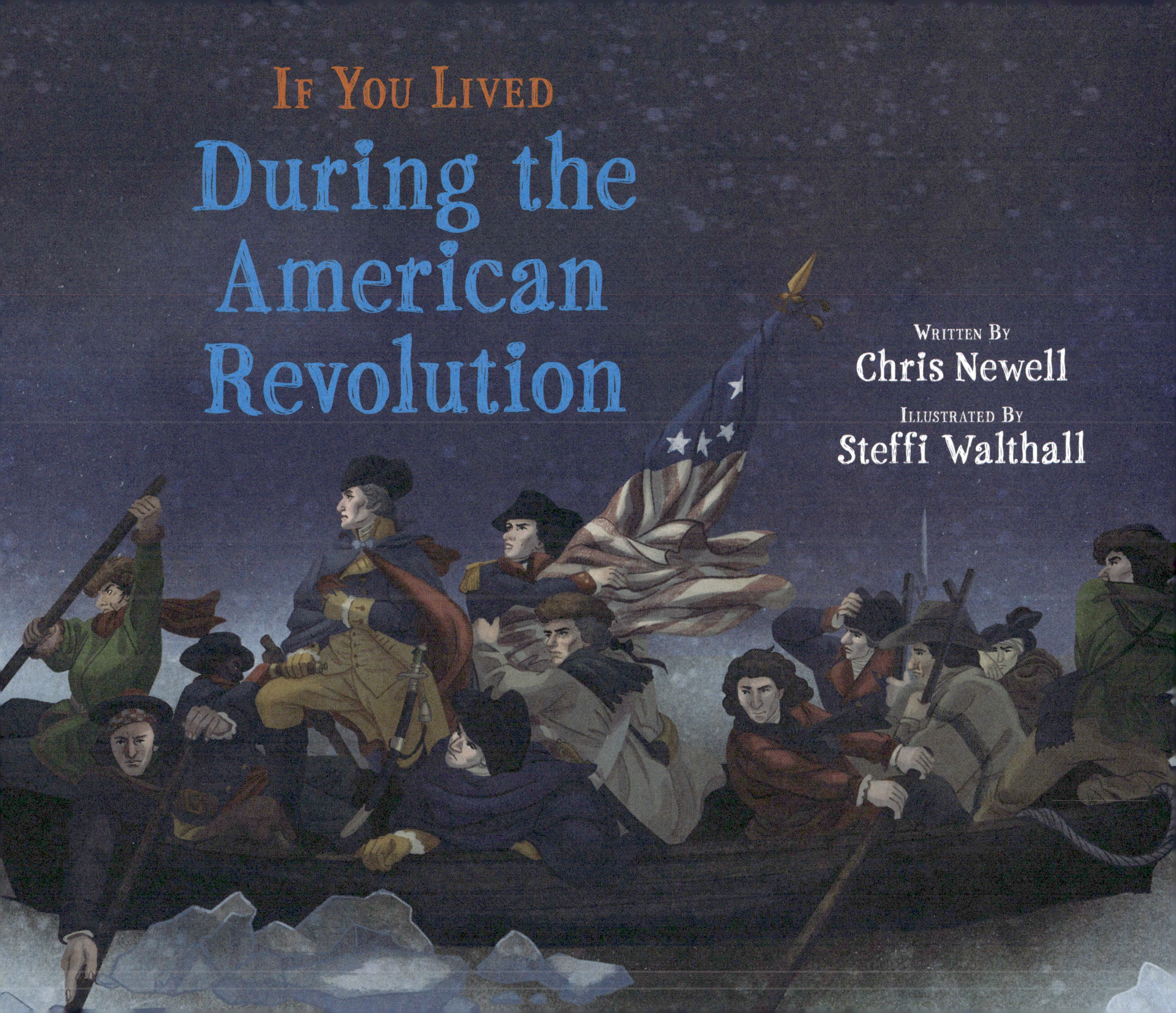

Table of Contents

Introduction

Colonization by European peoples of what we now call the United States of America began as early as the sixteenth century. The European countries of Spain, France, and England all staked claims on areas of the continent they sought to call their own. On the eastern coast of the continent, England's territory was divided into separate chartered colonies, all under the reign of the king of England.

When the first English colony was established in 1607, America was lush with old-growth forests and thriving fish and animal populations. These natural resources were seen as untapped by European powers. The harvesting of these resources and the introduction of crops like sugar made the Americas essential to the **economy** of the growing British Empire.

Colony founders engaged in contracts with their rulers. The colonists would harvest the natural resources and return them to England. In exchange, English law gave colonists a claim to the land they occupied. For a landless person from England, America held a promise of wealth from the **commodification** of its rich resources and the security of landownership, which the English valued above all else.

However, the settlement of the colonies was complex. Indigenous populations occupied, governed, and stewarded the lands the English wished to claim. As a result, the colonizing English made treaties on behalf of their king with leaders of Native populations. The English understood these treaties as a claim to the land and all its resources.

By the late eighteenth century, the situation had changed significantly. Different European interests led to armed conflict among Spain, France, and Great Britain on American soil. In addition, the colonies had tenuous and often volatile relationships with Native populations. This was due to the failure of English-led colonial governments to honor treaties and their willingness to encroach on Native territories and lifeways far beyond their original agreements.

The Seven Years' War, also known as the French and Indian War, began in 1754. It saw the French, French colonists in North America, and their Native allies battling for territory against Great Britain, English-speaking colonists, and the Haudenosaunee Confederacy (known at the time as the Iroquois Confederacy). The war ended in 1763 with significant British territory gains and debts from the war effort.

Great Britain's behavior toward the American colonies significantly changed in the decade following the war. Great Britain enacted policies and laws aimed at covering their war debt and avoiding another war with Native peoples west of the Appalachian Mountains. From 1764, the British began passing new tax laws, placing additional British troops within the colonies, and strictly enforcing British **imperialism**. This built resentment among colonists toward their British rulers.

By the 1770s, the relationship between the colonists and the British leadership had strained to the point of armed rebellion. Violence escalated into the American Revolution, a war for independence from British rule.

What was colonial America like in the 1700s?

Life in colonial America was very different from life in the United States we know today. Homes did not have electricity or running water. Ships sailed across the ocean. Native peoples outnumbered American colonists. Enslavement was accepted and practiced by colonizing countries worldwide, and not all people in America were free. Women, enslaved peoples from West Africa, and Native peoples of the Americas did not have the same rights as landowning, English-speaking men.

Indigenous cultures were the dominant populations of the continent. English-speaking colonists generally lived only in areas established through treaties with Native leaders. These treaties recognized colonial governing authority. However, these treaties were continuously violated by settlers. As a result, relationships between British colonies and Native populations ranged from cooperative to hostile, depending on the circumstances and the times.

Colonial Americans, enslaved people, and Native peoples alike did not depend on grocery stores. People often produced their own food, clothing, and shelter. The primary way of life for people in the Americas was **agriculture**. Most people had to grow and harvest their own food. As colonial settlement increased, the colonists required more farmland to feed their growing population.

While wealthy colonial Americans may have **imported** and worn clothing from Europe, families of lesser means often made their own clothes. Native peoples often traded for items like European cotton shirts and colorfully patterned cloth. It was not uncommon for them to wear traditional clothes made from animal hides as well as cotton or leather clothing items. Indigenous peoples also traded for practical items, like kettles, weapons, and gunpowder.

For shelter, Indigenous families continued to live traditionally in semipermanent structures constructed from the natural resources of their respective areas. Colonial Americans followed the footsteps of their English forebears and used lumber as construction material for structures occupied year-round such as homes and other buildings.

What is a colony?

A colony is a territory that has been settled by people from another country, and that is controlled by that country. Establishing a colony on behalf of a ruler was a way for Europeans to become wealthy landowners under European laws. Many settlements within colonies were established as **plantations**. The king or queen rewarded the colony founders with charters to rule the territories. In exchange, the founders shared the profits of selling the land-rich resources with the ruler. Settlers in these colonies made contracts with the colony founders. They would pay off their debts to the colony by producing and selling goods and resources.

What were the thirteen colonies?

The first English colony in the Americas was called Roanoke. It was established in a charter between Sir Walter Raleigh and Queen Elizabeth I in 1587. More than 100 total men, women, and children lived in the original colony. However, the colony failed, and by 1590 the original site of the Roanoke colony was found abandoned.

The first successful settlement for the English was Jamestown. It was on the Chesapeake Bay and would eventually become the Virginia colony. Initially settled with tales and promises of gold, the colony struggled until the colonists learned how to successfully cultivate and harvest tobacco from local Native peoples. This created an enormously booming economy based on the growth and **export** of tobacco back to Europe. After the success of Jamestown, more English colonies were established up and down the east coast of North America.

There were four main groups of colonies.

The New England Colonies included Massachusetts, New Hampshire, Connecticut, and Rhode Island Plantation.

The Middle Colonies were farther down the coast and included New York, New Jersey, Delaware, and Pennsylvania.

The Chesapeake Colonies included Virginia and Maryland.

The Southern Colonies comprised North Carolina, South Carolina, and Georgia.

How did the establishment of colonies change the landscape?

The land where the English established colonies was already occupied by various Indigenous cultures. These Native peoples often lived under sustainable notions of land stewardship, not ownership. Land stewardship meant that the land was not owned by individuals but taken care of by the community. This care included controlled burning of forest areas to prevent forest fires and make hunting easier. Fruiting trees were trimmed of dead branches to make their harvests more abundant. Agricultural practices were built on the cycles of nature and involved planting complementary crops, or crops of plants that help each other grow. Everyone had a hand in the caretaking of the land, and in return, the land provided abundant resources that ensured their survival.

Most English colonists had cultural and religious beliefs that humanity's duty was to "improve" land, which conflicted with Native land stewardship techniques and incentivized colonists to cut down trees and build year-round settlements in what they saw as untouched land. Concepts of *landownership* took over the concepts of land *stewardship* as colonies became overrun by English-speaking peoples in a rush for wealth and freedom in what Europeans called the New World.

By the time of the American Revolution, the land within the borders of the British colonies reflected English landownership values. Individuals owned property that was divided among landowners by boundary lines and fences, in contrast to the communal use of farmland practiced by Native cultures. Settlements became ports; ports became cities. Roads connected settlements, and profiting off the land instead of stewarding its resources became the way of life.

English colonies changed land-use patterns drastically. This permanently changed the landscape stewarded by Native peoples.

Who was a colonial American?

Providing an accurate description of a colonial American is a difficult task. Not all colonial Americans were from England. The first recorded usage of *America* appears in a 1507 map created by German cartographer Martin Waldseemüller, based on Italian explorer Amerigo Vespucci's mapping of South America and the Caribbean. By the late 1500s, it was common for Europeans to refer to anything from the American continent, or New World, as "American," including Native peoples, people from other continents born in America, and people who emigrated to America.

Many colonial Americans in the 1700s were people of European ancestry who had been born in America. However, African people, forcibly enslaved in the transatlantic slave trade, were brought to the English colonies as early as 1619. By the time of the American Revolution, generations of enslaved people were also part of colonial America. They were not free, and lived, worked, and died at the will of their enslavers. At the beginning of the American Revolution, slavery was legal in all thirteen colonies. Many free colonial Americans saw the practice as unjust, but many actively participated. People of non-European ancestry, both free and enslaved, also played a part in the events of the Revolution.

The most defining characteristic of colonial America was the use of the English language, making nearly all non-Indigenous colonial Americans part of the Anglophone, or English-speaking, cultures. As a result, English was the common language spoken by colonial Americans, and the country's founding documents are all written in English.

What was the Seven Years' War?

The Seven Years' War, also known as the French and Indian War, took place on the American continent from 1754 to 1763. It could be considered the first global war. What began as a North American territorial dispute between Britain and France expanded into a conflict that saw European nations at war on multiple continents with considerable costs.

Several interests led to the war. Though Native peoples already occupied the Ohio River Valley, the French laid claim to the territory. They wanted control over the region and exclusive rights to trade with Native peoples in the area. Great Britain wished to take over the Ohio River Valley and settle it with British colonists. The British outnumbered the French on the continent by a significant proportion. As a result, the British settlers' desire for more land fueled a territorial dispute that eventually became violent. Native peoples took sides with either the French or the British, depending on their interests. Due to their smaller numbers, the French relied heavily on their Native allies during the war.

The Haudenosaunee Confederacy in the north and Cherokee and Catawba peoples in the southern valley region sided with the British. The French were supported by some tribes of the Wabanaki Confederacy and other Algonquin-speaking peoples in the region such as the Lenape, Huron, Ojibway, and Ottawa peoples, as they had strong diplomatic ties with these groups.

Armed conflict began in the Ohio Valley region in 1752. Under the command of Charles Michel de Langlade, three hundred French Canadian soldiers and Ottawa warriors set out to punish the Miami people for breaking an agreement with the French and continuing to trade with the British. An attack on the Miami trading village Pickawillany resulted in the deaths of a few British traders and several Miami people.

Following this, the French fortified their positions in the valley and added thousands of troops. The inhabitants of the British colonies responded. In October 1753, Governor

Robert Dinwiddie of Virginia assigned a twenty-one-year-old named George Washington to lead a regiment and warn the French to leave Virginia territory. French commander Jacques Legardeur de Saint-Pierre refused to leave.

George Washington

Both sides prepared for war. The French constructed Fort Duquesne where the Allegheny and Monongahela Rivers meet. Following an early battle, Washington, now commissioned lieutenant colonel, built and commanded Fort Necessity in what is now Pennsylvania.

Many early campaigns were disastrous for the British. On July 3, 1754, the French successfully attacked Fort Necessity and took control. Washington found himself on the losing side of the conflict and negotiated a withdrawal.

In June 1755, an expedition set out to take over Fort Duquesne. It was led by Major General Edward Braddock, with Washington at his side. The British were soundly defeated, and the French successfully defended their fort.

General Braddock ordered a retreat before he lost his life. Washington led the retreat of around five hundred of Braddock's troops to Virginia.

Washington's campaign in the Ohio Valley destroyed several Haudenosaunee villages. This earned him the nickname "Town Destroyer," a name previously given to Washington's great-grandfather John Washington.

From 1756 to 1757, the French and their Native allies continued to win against the British. Then, in 1758, the British successfully blockaded French shipping into the St. Lawrence River, effectively cutting off supplies and reinforcements to all French territories.

Later that same year, the British seized territories in Nova Scotia from French rule. In the years following, the British took control of Fort Ticonderoga, in what is now New York State, as well as Fort Niagara. From 1760 through 1763, the war continued sporadically before coming to an end with the signing of the Treaty of Paris of 1763.

The treaty resulted in large territorial exchanges. The British had been successful in several campaigns into Canada, and France ceded, or gave up, all their claims in North America.

Native peoples in the region were heavily impacted by this treaty. Many tribes, unhappy with British occupation of their homelands, revolted against British settlements in 1763. This uprising was led by several tribal leaders, most notably Ottawa Chief Pontiac, and is now known as Pontiac's War. The campaign was unsuccessful at getting the British to permanently leave the territory.

CHIEF PONTIAC

The new land came at a cost. The war had been expensive, and maintaining a military presence in the region was a drain on the British economy. As a result, Great Britain decided to recover the costs of the war from the colonial Americans. This led to tension between colonial Americans and the British, which would eventually lead to more conflict.

What led up to the American Revolution?

After the Seven Years' War ended in 1763, several events planted the seeds of revolution for colonial Americans. The British had defeated the French and their allies, but the debt from the war was massive and would require payment for years to come. Britain's newly claimed territories in Canada were occupied by Native peoples who were not allied with or loyal to the British. As a result, the British felt the need to maintain a standing army in the Americas to convey the threat of violence.

Though the British claimed the Ohio River Valley after the war, the area was still occupied and controlled by Native

peoples. Chief Pontiac's War had tried to stop British territorial advancement in the area. Though the rebellion was unsuccessful at removing the British from the region, the resistance did lead to Britain's Proclamation of 1763, which forbade colonial Americans from settling the region west of the Appalachian Mountains.

Colonial Americans saw this as an overreach of British power. They had the intent and will to encroach on that territory regardless of Native occupation. Great Britain also used their military presence to tighten controls on

navigation and trade in American colonies. Considering the high cost of war and maintaining order, the British felt that the American colonists should pay for their own defense in the future. This led to several British **reforms** in the American colonies that caused first tension and then resistance by colonial Americans.

By the spring of 1772, bodies of representatives known as committees of correspondence had formed throughout the colonies, representing the move toward cooperation, action, and an emerging national identity as Americans, which divorced European American colonists from their European roots.

The committees of correspondence and colonial newspapers helped to persuade more American colonists to consider independence from British rule.

What was the American Revolution?

The American Revolution, also known as the Revolutionary War, took place from 1775 through 1783. Colonial Americans went to war against Great Britain to gain their independence and the ability to self-govern. This war began

in response to the British **enactment** of laws, tariffs, and other difficulties. Colonial Americans saw these laws as **tyrannical**. As a result, the thirteen American colonies banded together, declared their independence, and began armed conflict against the British.

During the war, colonial Americans allied with different groups of Native peoples and enslaved Africans. However, each group had different motivations for fighting. Colonists fought to free themselves from British rule, enslaved Black people fought for freedom, and their Indigenous allies fought to achieve peace in their homelands.

As a result of the American Revolution, an experiment in self-government began. A country was born out of fierce resistance, savvy military wit, new thinking, and the desire to move forward as united peoples with the promise of something better than before.

What was the Sugar Act of 1764?

Since its establishment, colonial America had been subject to English laws regulating trade and navigation. Before the Seven Years' War, many were not enforced. In fact, regulation was so lacking that colonial Americans carried on trade with French settlers after the war, upsetting the British rulers.

In 1764, the British **Parliament** passed the Sugar Act (or the American Revenue Act of 1764), a reform of a similar law called the Sugar and Molasses Act of 1733. Before this reform, many people were **smuggling** sugar and molasses into the Americas to avoid paying taxes. The New England regional economy was a large producer and exporter of rum,

which required sugar or molasses to make. Smuggled sugar could be purchased at a lower price, which made American rum more affordable.

The Sugar Act changed everything. The new Sugar Act lowered the taxes on sugar and molasses from British territories, but it also allowed **customs** agents to crack down on smuggled sugar from other territories. With the tax in place, producers were required to use the more expensive British sugar. American rum became more expensive and less desirable. The Sugar Act also banned the direct shipment of American goods such as lumber to European countries other than Great Britain. Additionally, the act included new taxes on imported foreign goods such as certain wines, coffee, and printed fabrics.

The first lord of the Treasury, George Grenville, increased the British navy's presence and installed a new system to enforce customs laws and strictly collect duties and taxes.

The newly enforced taxes had a negative domino effect on the colonial economy.

What was the Stamp Act of 1765?

In April 1763, Lord George Grenville assumed the role of first lord of the Treasury and prime minister of Great Britain. He expanded the taxation of the American colonies with the passage of the Stamp Act of 1765. The Stamp Act taxed nearly all forms of paper, from legal documents to newspapers and even playing cards.

The Stamp Act was passed by Parliament on March 22, 1765. A stamp tax was not uncommon in Britain at the time. However, this was the first direct tax on American colonial citizens.

Parliament had considered colonial stamp taxes several times but never imposed them. Grenville convinced Parliament to exercise their right, as he saw it, to tax the colonies directly.

The American colonies resisted immediately. Individual Americans such as Benjamin Franklin and political groups like the Sons of Liberty were part of a successful campaign of public revolt against the Stamp Act. America's reaction to the Stamp Act was so negative and forceful that tax commissioners quit their jobs out of fear. Benjamin Franklin said of the Stamp Act that Americans would never pay it "unless compelled by force of arms."

Britain's inability to enforce the Stamp Act led to its **repeal** on March 18, 1766. For American colonists, the victory against direct taxation gave them confidence that they could avoid such taxes in the future.

What other grievances did the American colonies have?

The repeal of the Stamp Act did not end American colonists' grievances with the British government. Britain continued to pass laws meant to exercise their control over the colonies. Unwilling to accept defeat after the repeal of the Stamp Act, British parliament passed the Declaratory Act asserting Britain's right to solely declare all laws for the American colonies, further expanding their control.

The Currency Act of 1764 took away the colonies' ability to trade with their own paper currency and required taxes from the Sugar Act be paid in gold. This made paper currency from the colonies essentially worthless.

The Quartering Act of 1765 forced colonial assemblies to house and supply British troops. American colonists already objected to having a standing British army in the colonies. Being forced to house and supply the British army felt like another tax to the colonists.

In 1767, the British parliament passed another law taxing British imports such as paper, glass, and tea as they arrived in American colonies. These were called the Townshend duties. These new duties were designed to raise money for the British treasury, and the American colonies alone paid them. American colonists saw the Townshend duties as another revenue-generating tax at their expense.

Some of the major port cities in the colonies resisted the Townshend duties. Boston was the home of many of the colonial disruptions to British rule. Boston was also the seat of a board of customs commission created by the British to impose tax laws and hold smugglers and anyone trying to avoid paying British taxes accountable. American colonists in Boston, and later Philadelphia and New York, arranged **boycotts** of taxed goods. The British posted four regiments of troops in Boston. The proximity of these opposing forces within the same city would soon lead to violence. Clashes in the streets between American colonists and British troops eventually led to the Boston Massacre in 1770.

What was the Boston Massacre?

The Boston Massacre was the first clash between American colonists and British troops resulting in casualties and deaths. Four regiments and a company of British troops in Boston totaled less than 2,000 soldiers in a city that housed approximately 15,500 colonists. Pay for British soldiers, known as British Regulars, was low. As a result, many of them took off-duty jobs in the city. The increased competition for work added another layer of resentment for Boston residents.

By 1770, American colonists were defining themselves by their loyalties, either to the American colonies or the British Crown, increasing tension in the colonies. This tension led to numerous skirmishes between colonists loyal to Great Britain and colonists who wanted to be free of British rule. Merchants loyal to the Crown saw their stores vandalized by other colonists under the rallying cry of "no taxation without representation." This meant the anti-British colonists refused to pay any taxes that were created without an elected representative speaking on behalf of the colonies.

These skirmishes were often violent. During one incident, a merchant trying to protect his store shot and killed a child. Afterward, tensions were at an all-time high. On March 5, 1770, a lone British soldier was guarding the

Boston Custom House, where the king's tax money was stored, when he was surrounded by a mob of anti-British colonists. When they began pelting the soldier with ice and snow, he called for reinforcements.

British Captain Thomas Preston arrived with a small

force of eight soldiers and four civilians and took a defensive position in front of the Boston Custom House. They were attacked with clubs and other blunt weapons. In the panic, a soldier fired his gun, causing the rest of the soldiers to open fire. Five American colonists died, including a mixed-race Indigenous and Black man named Crispus Attucks. The child of an enslaved father and a local Natick Praying Indian mother, he is known as the first casualty of the American Revolution.

Much is still unclear about the Boston Massacre. No one knows if the first gunshot was intentional. Captain Preston and the other soldiers were prosecuted by the British after the massacre. British troops quickly retreated out of the city.

While the violence that led to the death of five Bostonians began with the colonists, the loss of their comrades became part of the rallying cry against British soldiers. Paul Revere depicted British soldiers murdering American colonists in a famous etching that portrayed the colonists as defenseless gentlemen and the British soldiers as cruel and brutal.

What was the Boston Tea Party?

In 1773, Parliament enacted the Tea Act. While the tax on tea from the Townshend duties was still active, the Tea Act was meant to raise money for the East India Company by giving them a **monopoly** on selling tea in the colonies. The British assumed that the act would lower the price of tea for the colonies. However, given the sentiment of American colonists toward any British taxation, the Tea Act spurred the American colonists' most well-known act of rebellion—the Boston Tea Party.

With this new tax, the boycotts on British goods intensified. Previous uprisings of rebellion had been small and local. The tea boycott was different. Spurred on by years of anti-British sentiment against corrupt and tyrannical leaders, the boycott gained momentum over a large swath of American colonial society.

Leaders in many colonies decided to prevent East India Company ships from docking at their ports. If they could not unload their cargo, they would be forced to return the tea to England. Though some cities were able to turn the ships away, three tea ships arrived in Boston and would not leave.

On December 16, 1773, a group of fifty to sixty men disguised themselves as Indigenous people to **dissociate** their appearance from Boston townspeople. They boarded the three East India Company ships, broke open the cargo

holds, and dumped all the tea stored inside into the harbor as an act of protest. News of the "tea party" in Boston spread through the colonies, inspiring similar acts of rebellion.

From this moment, the relationship between Great Britain and its American colonies changed forever. Response from the British arrived through four new laws, known to them as the Coercive Acts. To the Americans, they would come to be known as the Intolerable Acts.

What were the Coercive Acts?

The Coercive Acts were a set of laws passed by Parliament in 1774 to quell the "commotions and insurrections" that were taking place in Massachusetts and other colonies. Despite the widespread nature of the tea protests, Boston was a big player in the insurrection, so Boston became the target for **retribution**.

On June 1, 1774, British Parliament closed the Boston port with the **Boston Port Act**. Later that summer, they enacted the Administration of Justice Act and the Massachusetts Government Act.

The **Administration of Justice Act** ensured a fair trial for British officials charged with capital offenses while upholding the law or quelling protests in the Massachusetts Bay Colony. American colonists saw this act as legalizing the murder of colonists who rebelled against the Crown. They called it the Murder Act.

The **Massachusetts Government Act** changed how the

Massachusetts Bay Colony would be governed. It did away with the colony's charter. The right to vote for the executive council was withdrawn and the king now appointed all council members. Along with these changes, having more than one town meeting a year was forbidden without the governor's permission.

These three acts, combined with a new Quartering Act, which resembled the one previously established in 1765, were considered intolerable by American colonists and their leaders. Britain's rule was seen as increasingly tyrannical. In response, colonists organized the First Continental Congress to coordinate their protest.

What was the First Continental Congress?

The First Continental Congress was the body of delegates, or representatives, who spoke and acted collectively for the colonies. After Britain passed the Coercive Acts, fifty-six deputies representing every colony except Georgia met on September 5, 1774, in Carpenters' Hall in Philadelphia, Pennsylvania.

The congress met in secret. Each colony had one vote per issue, giving each equal representation. They passed a document called the Declaration and Resolves, which stated familiar individual rights we have today such as life, liberty, property, assembly, and trial by jury. The First Continental Congress **denounced** the notion of taxation without representation and the continued presence and maintenance of British forces in the colonies.

The First Continental Congress also demanded the British Crown rectify the injustices that began in 1763. To reinforce their demands, they agreed to boycott all imported and exported British goods except rice if the British allowed the injustices to continue.

Finally, they decided to meet again on May 10, 1775, to consider the next steps.

How did the American Revolutionary War begin?

By 1775, the American colonies were under the leadership of the Continental Congress and were beginning steps toward independence. The Continental Congress approved preparations for armed conflict. These preparations lasted several months.

General Thomas Gage, commander of the British troops in Boston, received an order to arrest Continental Congress

members Samuel Adams and John Hancock. Both men were targeted, as they were important figures to the American colonists in the decade leading up to the Revolution. They are also now seen as founding fathers of the United States of America. As a political leader, Samuel Adams was a key figure in the Revolution. John Hancock would rise to become president of the Continental Congress.

About seven hundred British troops were dispatched from Boston on April 18, 1775, to Lexington, Massachusetts, where Adams and Hancock were believed to be. The British

also had orders to seize weapons and gunpowder stockpiled by the American colonists in Concord, Massachusetts.

However, the Continental Army kept a watchful eye on British troop activity. Patriots William Dawes and Paul Revere rode out from Boston to warn colonists that the British were coming. Paul Revere's efforts to warn colonists are famously recorded in Henry Wadsworth Longfellow's poem *Paul Revere's Ride*.

On April 19, 1775, the first armed conflict between colonists and British redcoats took place. British troops arrived in Lexington and were engaged by dozens of colonial minutemen.

The following skirmish resulted in eight dead minutemen and over a dozen wounded.

From Lexington, the British troops marched on Concord to destroy what was left of a cache of weapons and gunpowder. However, when they arrived, they found most of the stock of guns and gunpowder already gone due to the swift action of the Continental Army. The skirmish in

Concord resulted in what is now famously known as "the shot heard 'round the world."

These encounters became known as the Battles of Lexington and Concord. Regardless of who fired the first shot, rebelling colonists were the first to get their version of events out by utilizing printing presses and colonial newspapers.

Armed conflict between Great Britain and the American colonists was well underway. The Continental Congress would have to manage the conflict.

The policymakers in Great Britain continued to try to enforce dominance over the colonies. Over the next year, they tried to recruit Native peoples, mercenaries, and enslaved people to join them against the colonists. The British blockaded ports, disrupting more trade. Both sides shot down any attempt at settling the conflict through diplomacy. By the end of the year, many members of the Continental Congress favored the fight for independence.

What is a patriot?

A patriot is a person who vigorously supports their country and is prepared to defend it from opponents. Before the American Revolution, the king of Great Britain controlled the thirteen colonies. The land and the people living in those colonies were subject to his rule. However, by the mid-1700s, generations of colonial Americans had been born on American soil. Though they owned land in America under laws established by Great Britain, they developed a growing loyalty to the land where they were born. American patriots no longer considered England a homeland. As a result, they felt a growing sense of loyalty to their colonial leaders instead of the king. During this time, patriots were the people during the American Revolution who fought for colonial America's independence from British rule.

What is a loyalist?

A loyalist is a person who remains loyal to the established ruler. American loyalists were colonial Americans who remained faithful to the king of Great Britain. There were numerous reasons why some colonial Americans preferred British rule. Most colonial Americans were of British descent and still had family and relatives in England. Trade connections, loyalty to the Church of England, and local rivalries could all contribute to individual allegiances. The thirteen colonies owed their existence to both funding from Great Britain and long-term protection by British military forces.

Many loyalists saw Great Britain's well-developed military and concluded that a war with Great Britain would be very costly in both wealth and lives lost. During the American Revolution, about one in five colonial Americans were loyalists.

What was Paul Revere's Ride?

Paul Revere is often considered a folk hero of the American Revolution. He is known primarily for his famous midnight ride from Boston to Lexington in 1775 to warn John Hancock and Samuel Adams that the British were marching on Lexington.

PAUL REVERE

Born in the North End of Boston in 1734, Revere was educated at the North Writing School. In 1773, he joined the Boston Committee of Correspondence and in 1774, the Massachusetts Committee of Safety as an express rider in charge of carrying news, messages, and important documents as far as New York City and Philadelphia.

His famous midnight ride began around 10:00 p.m. on the evening of April 18, 1775. Summoned by Dr. Joseph Warren, Revere was tasked with riding from Boston to Lexington to warn John Hancock and Samuel Adams that

British troops in Boston were mobilizing. Warren believed the British planned to march on Lexington with the aim of capturing both men. He also thought the British might seize the arms stored in the town of Concord.

There were two possible routes to Lexington. One crossed the Charles River by boat. The other was a march by land across Boston Neck. It had been predetermined by the Sons of Liberty that a signal from the steeple of Christ Church, also known as Old North Church, in the North End of Boston would signify which path the British had taken. Two lanterns meant a British approach over water. A single lantern signified a British approach by land. As Revere set out on his journey that evening, he instructed a fellow patriot to light two lanterns.

Revere stopped at his house to get his boots and overcoat. From there, he went to the waterfront at the North End of Boston where two friends were waiting to ferry him across the Charles River. He landed successfully and confirmed with other local Sons of Liberty that they had seen the signal alerting to a water crossing from Christ Church.

Around 11:00 p.m., he borrowed a horse and began the famous ride to Lexington. He was nearly captured just outside Charlestown and altered his route through the village of Medford. There, he informed the local militia of the movements of the British.

Avoiding the homes of known loyalists, Revere arrived

in Lexington just after midnight to deliver his message to John Hancock, who was still awake. From there, Revere joined another messenger named William Dawes and rode on to Concord to warn the town.

They did not make it. A short distance from Lexington, they were captured by British troops, along with a high-ranking member of the Sons of Liberty named Dr. Samuel Prescott. Both Prescott and Dawes escaped and were able to warn Concord and Lexington. Revere was held for questioning and later released. However, his horse was confiscated, and he had to walk back to Lexington on foot, arriving near the end of the battle.

Though he never reached Concord, the main objectives of Revere's ride were met. Samuel Adams and John Hancock had been warned about their impending capture. They were able to "alarm the countryside." The message was delivered, and Adams and Hancock were not captured.

What was the Second Continental Congress?

The Second Continental Congress was the representative body of delegates that led the colonies during the war. They first met at the State House in Philadelphia in May 1775. New delegates to the Continental Congress included Benjamin Franklin and Thomas Jefferson, who would become important figures in the establishment of the new country.

By the time they met on May 10, battles between colonial Americans and British soldiers had already broken out in the Massachusetts towns of Lexington and Concord. The Second Continental Congress began by adopting a militia force from the New England colonies as its army—the militia assembled around Boston—and appointed George Washington as commander in chief on June 15, 1775. A June 16, 1775, entry from the Journals of the Continental Congress says

> *. . . that the Congress had by a unanimous vote made choice of him to be general and com[mander] in chief to take the supreme command of the forces raised and to be*

raised, in defence of American Liberty, and desired his acceptance of it.

With the Continental Army now under General Washington's command, the Second Continental Congress served as the provisional, or temporary, government of the United Colonies.

As a government, they elected a president of Congress, issued and borrowed money, established a postal service, and created a military that included a navy and an army known as the Continental Army. The Second Continental Congress argued for cutting ties with the British. On July 2, 1776, with New York initially **abstaining**, twelve of the thirteen colonies unanimously resolved that the United Colonies had the right to be free and independent states. On July 4, 1776, they approved the Declaration of Independence, officially cutting all ties with Great Britain and claiming the rights of self-government. Colonial Americans were now officially in a struggle for true independence.

What was the Continental Army like?

George Washington accepted his appointment as commander in chief of the Continental Army, telling Congress the following:

> *Tho' I am truly sensible of the high Honour done me in this Appointment, yet I feel great distress, from a consciousness that my abilities and Military experience may not be equal to the extensive and important Trust . . .*
>
> *But lest some unlucky event should happen unfavourable to my reputation, I beg it may be remembered by every Gentleman in the room, that I this day declare with the utmost sincerity, I do not think my self equal to the Command I am honored with.*

George Washington proved to be a wise military leader. Recognizing that the militia force from New England was no match for British Regulars, General Washington took on the difficult work of building a true Continental Army.

When speaking of Washington's strategy, his future aide Alexander Hamilton later said "our hopes are not placed in any particular city or spot of ground, but in preserving a good army . . . to take advantage of favorable opportunities, and waste and defeat the enemy by piecemeal."

Preserving a "good army" meant an adequately trained and armed force that was fully supplied and organized. Some of the army's soldiers had experience from the Seven Years' War, but their numbers were small. Many of the Continental Army recruits were young and inexperienced. Soldiers ranged in age from sixteen (or fifteen, with a parent's permission) to fifty-five.

During the war, a total of around 230,000 soldiers served in the Continental Army, but never more than 48,000 at one time. They were **supplemented** by 145,000 militia members. Continental Army soldiers were paid a monthly wage. Privates made around $6.25 a month. On top of that, each soldier was given a ration of beef, fish, or pork daily, along with bread or flour, dried vegetables, milk, and hard cider or spruce beer.

By 1779, George Washington had standardized the Continental Army's uniform. Soldiers wore white or off-white breeches (short pants of the time fastened just below the knee); white waistcoats, or vests; and long blue jackets. The front of the jackets had colors representing the state the soldier's unit came from. The blue of the uniform earned Continental Army soldiers the nickname "bluecoats," which mimicked the nickname "redcoats" for British soldiers in reference to the red color of their jackets.

What was the Battle of Bunker Hill?

When violence broke out in 1775, the British were relentless in their attempts to end any thoughts of American independence. Despite this, the American colonists were getting more organized. While the Continental Army was largely inexperienced compared to British Regulars, they were highly motivated.

The first major action between American and British forces occurred at the Battle of Bunker Hill on June 17, 1775. As George Washington was in Philadelphia accepting the role of commander in chief of the newly formed Continental Army, the army was facing its first major confrontation with the British. They were under the command of Artemas Ward, who had served as commander-in-chief before George Washington took over.

The British took up positions near the Massachusetts towns of Dorchester and Charlestown Heights in preparation to invade on June 18. The colonists discovered their plans. Arriving on June 16, the Continental Army set up a defensible position on high ground nearby at Bunker Hill and Breed's Hill.

Due to poor health, Artemas Ward commanded the forces from his headquarters in Cambridge. He relied on the on-field command of Colonel William Prescott, a veteran leader during the Seven Years' War. Prescott would lead a provincial force of militiamen on the battlefields in and around Breed's Hill and Bunker Hill. This arrangement created miscommunications, which led to gaps in field command. For example, Ward commanded that Bunker Hill be fortified before the engagement. It's unclear whether Colonel Prescott ignored the order or simply chose the wrong hill, but the Continental Army instead built an earthen fort on nearby Breed's Hill, which was closer to the British position. The provincial force also created fortified firing positions on both hills. The higher ground proved essential to driving back British forces on two separate charges.

While Bunker Hill was eventually taken and held by the

British for much of the war, the resistance they encountered from American forces made this one of the bloodiest battles of the Revolution. Of the 2,300 British Regulars, officers, and marines, almost half were killed or wounded. Of the approximately 1,500 Continental soldiers who fought in the battle, somewhere between 300 and 500 were killed, wounded, or captured.

What is the Declaration of Independence?

In July 1776, after a decade of tension and distress over taxation and more than a year of war, the Second Continental Congress adopted the Declaration of Independence. This document laid out the multitude of grievances the American colonies had with their former British rulers, and officially declared the colonies free and independent from King George III's rule.

The Declaration of Independence was not a legally binding document. It was the document that *began* the process of legally recognized sovereignty, or the right to rule oneself, for American colonists.

Naming the new nation the United Colonies, the Declaration of Independence announced that all thirteen American colonies were officially separated from Great Britain. It resolves "That these United Colonies are, and of Right ought to be Free and Independent States."

A committee of five men wrote the Declaration. John

Adams of Massachusetts and Roger Sherman of Connecticut represented the New England colonies. Benjamin Franklin of Pennsylvania and Robert R. Livingston of New York represented the middle colonies, and the southern colonies were represented by Thomas Jefferson of Virginia, who wrote the draft currently housed in the Library of Congress.

The Declaration of Independence has five parts. An introduction, a preamble, the body in two sections, and a conclusion. The introduction is a declaration about the purpose of the document itself, which is to declare the causes that made it unavoidable and necessary for American colonies to separate from Great Britain.

The preamble is the most memorable part of the Declaration as it lays out principles considered "self-evident" by both Americans and British of the time. In part, it reads:

We hold these truths to be self-evident, that all men are created equal, that they

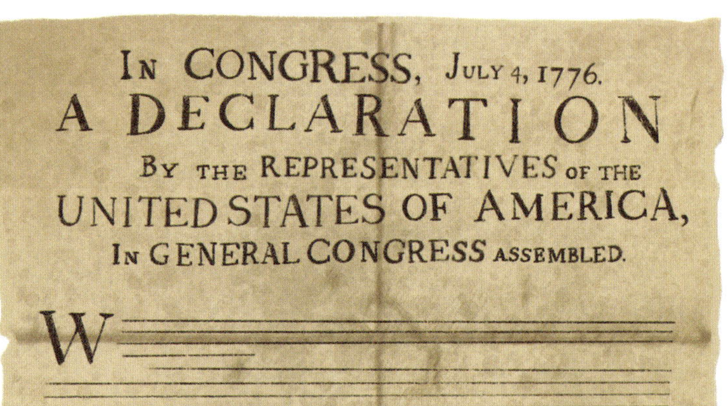

are endowed by their Creator with certain unalienable Rights, that among these are Life, Liberty and the pursuit of Happiness.

The first part of the body explains a long list of complaints and usurpations against the British government. These complaints include the following: not creating laws or allowing laws to be created for the public good; interference in elections; not administering justice in the colonies; appointing judges to the courts loyal only to the king; altering colonial governments; imposing taxes without consent; denying trial by jury; declaring war on the colonies; and many other injuries and usurpations.

The second part of the body explains that their appeals for "redress of their grievances" from Great Britain were in vain. All these factors together created the necessary conditions for American separation from King George III and Great Britain.

Having made their case for separation and independence in detail, the Declaration concludes: "That these United

Colonies are, and of Right ought to be Free and Independent States; that they are Absolved from all Allegiance to the British Crown, and that all political connection between them and the State of Great Britain, is and ought to be totally dissolved."

The Second Continental Congress voted on the declaration on July 2, 1776, and adopted the declaration on July 4, 1776. By September of 1776, the United Colonies adopted the name United States.

DID YOU KNOW?

The Declaration also blames Great Britain for inciting insurrections inside the colonies and turning the "merciless Indian Savages" against them. Ironically, while the writers of the Declaration of Independence paint Native peoples as bloodthirsty and merciless enemies, the United Colonies would call upon the help of Native peoples within fifteen days of adopting the Declaration of Independence in the Treaty of Watertown of 1776. This "treaty of alliance and friendship" between the United Colonies and the St. John's Indians (Maliseet) and Mi'kmaq peoples asking for help in the war to secure what General Washington called the "northern border." This is the first treaty to recognize the sovereignty of the United States as an independent nation.

What are the Articles of Confederation?

The Articles of Confederation were the first constitution of the new nation. The Continental Congress remained the government of the United States throughout the Revolutionary War, adopting the Articles of Confederation on November 15, 1777. Once adopted, the Continental Congress became known as the Confederation Congress. The Articles of Confederation established a "league of friendship" between the thirteen independent states. While adopted by Congress in 1777, the Articles were not official until sanctioned by all thirteen colonies on March 1, 1781.

The Articles of Confederation did not last. They structured the colonies very differently from the United States of America we know today. Under the Articles of Confederation, colonies become free and independent states. Still, with the lack of a strong centralized government, the states often found themselves in disputes over territory, taxation, and trade, among other disagreements, with no one to settle things. As a result, the United States of America was not very united and was advancing toward a complete collapse.

In May 1787, the Constitutional Convention met in the State House in Philadelphia. The windows were shuttered, and the delegates were sworn to secrecy. In mid-June, they decided to redesign the government entirely and

began the three-month process of writing the United States Constitution.

What happened to enslaved people during the war?

Enslaved people took different sides, depending on their circumstances. Enslavement was legal in all thirteen American colonies. The British did not initially intend to create a force of Black loyalist soldiers. However, Virginia became volatile during 1775, and the need to raise a sufficient army forced their hand. In November 1775, John Murray, the Earl of Dunmore, and the last royal British governor for the colony of Virginia, issued a proclamation offering freedom to enslaved or indentured Black rebels in return for their service in the British armed forces.

He wrote, "I do hereby farther declare all indented [sic] servants, Negroes, or others (appertaining to rebels) free, that are able and willing to bear arms, they joining his Majesty's troops, as soon as may be, for the more speedily reducing this colony to a proper sense of their duty, to his Majesty's crown and dignity."

In some ways, the proclamation was an act of desperation by Lord Dunmore, but it successfully recruited Black soldiers by the hundreds.

Even with this arrangement, both sides continued to enslave Black people who would not fight. General Washington was somewhat ambivalent about recruiting Black soldiers to fight for the Americans. He did not prioritize the recruitment of Black soldiers as the British had prioritized recruiting Black loyalists. However, as many as five thousand Black patriots fought for American independence and freedom in the Continental Army, while more served in the navy. For most Black patriot soldiers, fighting for the Continental Army helped them gain their freedom, though that was not the case for all who enlisted. Some Black American Revolutionary veterans would remain in bondage after their service.

Trained as soldiers and fighting on all fronts, enslaved Black people in the Americas fought for an outcome that might include their freedom.

What contributions did Indigenous peoples make to the Revolution?

General Washington was aware that the insufficient size of his force and the large geographic area they needed to defend was too much for the Continental Army to handle alone. Wabanaki peoples in what is now Maine were sympathetic to the American cause. They were invaluable in preserving the border to the north.

Not all Native peoples wanted to be involved in another conflict. Many saw the Revolution as infighting among the British. The Haudenosaunee tribes split in their decision to support the American colonists. The Oneida and Tuscarora peoples found themselves fighting on the side of the revolutionaries while other Haudenosaunee tribes stayed out of the battle or supported the English.

George Washington used the promise of money to entice even more assistance from Native peoples. The Passamaquoddy, Oneida, and Tuscarora were all offered money for their military service. Unfortunately, Native peoples who did not respond to George Washington's call for help were often seen as enemies to the American cause. In December 1776, Washington sent a dire warning to the Passamaquoddy chiefs:

Our Bretheren of the Six Nations and their Allies the Shawanese and Delewares would not hearken to the Advice of the Messengers sent among them but kept fast hold of our Ancient Covenant Chain; The Cherokees and the Southern Tribes were foolish enough to listen to them, and to take up the Hatchet Against us, Upon this our Warriours went into their Country, burnt their Houses, destroyed their Corn, and Oblidged them to sue for peace and give Hostages for their future Good Behaviour.

In the end, Native peoples who didn't help became enemies of the new government. For those who did help, all promises including payments were broken by the new United States government and its first president, George Washington.

What were the key moments of the Revolutionary War?

March 23, 1775: Virginian Patrick Henry, believing a war for independence was inevitable, strongly advocated for the arming of the Virginian militia in a famous speech. He is quoted as saying, "I know not what course others may take, but as for me, give me liberty or give me death!"

April 18–19, 1775: Paul Revere, Samuel Prescott, and William Dawes made their famous rides to warn that the British were on the march. The first shot of the war rang out at the Battles of Lexington and Concord, beginning hostilities between American rebels and the British.

June 17, 1775: Americans sieged British soldiers at the Battle of Bunker Hill. The British eventually took the hills above Charleston, but lost nearly half of their soldiers. The loss was not a military victory for the outnumbered Americans, but a moral victory.

January 1776: Thomas Paine published the pamphlet

Common Sense. Elegantly written in direct language, it sold thousands of copies. This pamphlet reframed the war as a war between separate nations and paved the way for the Declaration of Independence later that year.

February 27, 1776: An American force took on a unit of British loyalists (mostly Scotsmen) at Moores Creek Bridge in North Carolina. In the first major victory for the American army, the loyalists were defeated as they charged one thousand Continental Army soldiers assembled in a heavily fortified firing line over the bridge.

June 28, 1776: The American army won another battle in South Carolina. British forces, intending to invade Charleston via Sullivan's Island in Charleston Harbor, engaged in an all-day attack. They were pushed back without a single British soldier stepping foot on land. The invading army turned around in defeat.

July 4, 1776: America declared its independence from Great Britain.

September 15, 1776: Due to miscommunication between the Americans and clever timing from the British, George Washington's forces are unable to stop invading British forces at the Battle of Kip's Bay. They lose a significant part of New York City to the British.

November 16, 1776: General Washington suffered another defeat at Fort Washington on Manhattan Island. The fort was thought to be invulnerable. However, in a

devastating loss for the Americans, the British attacked the fort from multiple sides and earned another victory against Washington's forces.

December 25–26, 1776: After being driven across New Jersey into Pennsylvania by the British, Continental Army soldiers struck back by secretly crossing the Delaware River to Trenton. They surprised a garrison of British troops at dawn, taking nine hundred prisoners.

September 19–October 7, 1777: The Battle of Saratoga was one of the most decisive battles of the war. The American army forced British General John Burgoyne to surrender, stopping the advance of the British in the Hudson River Valley. As a result of this battle, France signed a treaty with the United States. This treaty secured the financing and military support for the Americans from the French.

December 19, 1777–June 19, 1778: Washington and his soldiers spent the winter at Valley Forge, about twenty miles from British-occupied Philadelphia. Though the camp suffered greatly with illness, the soldiers who survived the winter emerged a well-trained and efficient fighting force.

February 6, 1778: France and the United States sign the Treaty of Amity and Commerce and the Treaty of Alliance. Up until this point the French had been secretly supplying Continental Army forces. These treaties paved the way for the mobilization of French soldiers and the French navy against the British. The full declaration of war by France against the British didn't come until June 1778.

March 1, 1781: The Articles of Confederation were ratified. While ultimately unsuccessful, adopting the Articles of Confederation was the first time the Americans declared their own national system of governance.

September–October 1781: The Siege at Yorktown took place. In March, many of the British forces had merged and set up a base in Yorktown, Virginia. General Washington and the French took this as an opportunity to besiege the fortifications, preventing food and supplies from entering.

October 18, 1781: British leader Lord Charles Cornwallis surrendered more than seven thousand soldiers to the Americans. This effectively ended land fighting. However, Americans, their allies, and British forces would continue to battle at sea.

September 3, 1783: The Treaty of Paris ended the war. The British accepted American independence and recognized United States borders, which included lands west of the Mississippi, although no arrangement with Native peoples of that region had yet been made.

Conclusion

The people living during the American Revolution saw drastic changes to their daily lives. Undermanned, underequipped, and underfunded populations of people came together for a common cause and won. The British colonies in America successfully declared and defended their independence from British rule. This changed the entire landscape for all peoples living on the continent whether they were Indigenous peoples, enslaved Black people, or

colonial European Americans. Each person who fought had their own reasons for joining the revolution.

The colonies achieved independence and made a new government and a new nation. However, Native peoples who helped the Americans saw promises made in treaties broken by the new government. Indigenous peoples who did not aid the revolution often suffered at the hands of the Continental Army during the war. After the war, they were treated as conquered peoples. Enslavement of Black people

continued long after the war. Under this new government, not all people were free.

As imperfect as the United States' origins are, the quest to form "a more perfect union" continues. The greatest wisdom shared by the people who founded the country was the knowledge that they couldn't govern the future. Therefore, they created a government by the people and for the people that could change and improve as humanity improves. We can accept the truth that this country was built on great things like the ideas of liberty and freedom but also relied on abominations such as the forced labor of enslaved people and the conquering of land occupied by Indigenous peoples to fuel the demands of ongoing colonialism.

The United States continues to grow and improve. The lofty goals of a country that recognizes that all people "are created equal" and works for the will of all its peoples continue to see progress. We are not a perfect union. However, we can continue to strive to be more perfect as a union, the promise the United States was built on.

Glossary

Abstaining: not participating in something, such as a vote or a discussion

Agriculture: the raising of crops and animals; farming

Boycott: to refuse to buy something or do business with someone as a punishment or protest

Commodification: the process of buying or processing raw agricultural materials

Customs: a place at a country's borders or ports where officials monitor what is brought into the country

Denounced: said in public that something was wrong or that someone did something wrong

Dissociate: to declare that one is not connected or a supporter of something

Economy: the system of buying, selling, making things, and managing money in a place

Enactment: the process of passing legislation

Export: to send products to another territory to sell them there

Imperialism: a policy of extending a country's power and influence beyond its borders, through diplomacy or military force

Imported: brought into a territory from somewhere else

Monopoly: the complete possession or control of the supply of a product or service

Parliament: the name that some countries use for the group of people who have been elected to make the laws

Plantation: a large farm found in warm climates where crops such as coffee, tobacco, and sugar are grown

Reform: an improvement or correction of something

Repeal: to officially cancel or otherwise do away with something, such as a law

Retribution: punishment inflicted on someone as revenge

Smuggling: moving goods illegally

Supplemented: added to something to complete it or to make up for what was missing

Tyrannical: exercising power over a small group through harsh enforcement of unfair laws